Chad's Playbook To Effective Leadership

Second Edition

Chad D. Bumgarner

ISBN: 0692519343
ISBN-13: 978-0692519349

DEDICATION

To my mother, Terlene Bumgarner, I love you darling! To my three beautiful daughters: Kharri, Courtney and Camryn, please understand that this is proof that you can do anything you want in this life with a little faith and a lot of hard work. To Dr. Kail, for your support and encouragement.

You sir, are an awesome mentor!!

ACKNOWLEDGEMENTS

First of all, I would like to thank Almighty God for giving me this message and platform.

I am blessed and excited to be able to write this book and share my thoughts and insight about leadership with the world.

I would like to thank my wife, Rosemarie, who is my rock and biggest supporter. She gave me the idea and the extra push to venture out into writing my very first book. Love you babe!!

I want to also thank my brother Lee Bumgarner for believing in me and knowing that I could complete such an accomplishment.

Thanks to my Organizational Leadership advisors and classmates at Mercer University, who consistently challenged me to work harder, dig deeper and to never stop learning!

Thanks to Nancy Cherry, Garion Bunn, Joseph Devon Cange, Keyaan Williams, Dr. Betsy Johnson, and my best friend for over twenty-five years, Thomas Surratt.

All of your words of wisdom, love and support mean more to me than you will ever know.

I'd also like to thank my classmates of '91 (Hickory High School). I truly believe that we are closer to each other than any other class that ever came out of HHS!

I really want to thank my mentor, Dr. John L. Mason. You have opened my eyes and helped me to see the leader that you see in me. Thank you for your guidance, patience and understanding. No rest for the weary! We've got more work to do!

Last but not least, I want to thank my dad, Douglas Bumgarner for always being in my corner – full of support, love and advice. I love and salute you. Thanks for being my Superman!!

Good Day Leaders,

I want to thank you from the bottom of my heart for purchasing my playbook for effective leadership! I applaud the fact that you took a personal approach to become a better and more effective leader. This will be a great opportunity for you to really examine yourself and see who you are as a leader as well as your flaws so that you can understand what you need to work on to be the leader that people WANT to follow.

I strongly urge you get the most out of the questions located at the end of each section. In order to do so, you will need to engage the experience with an open mind and answer the questions with a bit of curiosity. This is your chance to really explore and dig deep. There's no greater investment you can make than the ones you make in your life and your future. Take your time when reading and answering the questions while encouraging others who may be going through the text with you. In doing so, I believe you will enjoy the experience of what it's like to be a part of a community of fellow leaders.

Now it's obvious that this book won't be able to teach you everything you need to know about leadership in just a few hours, but doing this with others will help you to take a peek into new and different mindsets and beliefs of other leaders. This should give you some insight as to how your views and beliefs are impacting your team, company and goals. It's also a great way to increase your network!

Have some fun answering the questions and make it a point to stretch yourselves a bit more and step out of your comfort zone. In order for you to grow, lead and influence effectively and efficiently, it's going to take some work on your part. Are you ready? Let's GO!!

Best wishes,

Chad D. Bumgarner

Chad D. Bumgarner

INTRODUCTION

Many of us go to work every day and wonder how in the heck our bosses got promoted to their positions! There are many people today who are in positions of leadership, but can't lead their way out of a potato chip bag!

Millions of people encounter these issues every day on their jobs and unfortunately have to endure the inconsistent or lack of appropriate "leadership know-how," from their bosses.

Most of the time when people quit, they really leave their managers and not the job itself. In other words, when people leave for another job, it's because they probably can't continue to deal with their manager's management style any longer. It doesn't take much to become a great and effective leader for your team or employees. There is no magic pill or top secret formula of some sort. There are just **4 basic steps** that I have put together to help leaders – no matter what aspect you are leading in.

Leadership is all about effectively using your influence on others to achieve a mission or a goal. With my **4 steps**, I will show you how to lead your team, staff, etc.. effectively and positively. I want you to have a team that has amazing synergy, with you at the help. Using these steps, you will have a high-performing team in no time!

To the existing and potential leaders reading this book, before we get started, I would like to point out; in order to be an effective leader, you MUST:

Know who you are. You have to understand your strengths and weaknesses. You have to understand what your morals and beliefs are. Know absolutely what you WILL and WILL NOT budge on or take from anyone. What ideas and beliefs are you willing to fight for and defend to the end?

Standing firm on these positions will create confidence and trust with your followers; staff or employees. They will find you appealing and want to flock to you because you are showing transparency about who you are, and what you stand for.

Now, once you've figured out all of that, use my **4 steps** to become the leader that employees and staff dream about!

Before we get into the steps, let me just tell you that I enjoy using my past experiences to provide information that will make someone else a better leader.

The experience that led me to these 4 steps was a conversation I had with an older gentleman about the game of football. I'm a huge fan of the sport and so I love to talk about the great players and teams of the past and present. This particular time I was talking to this gentleman about great high school football teams of the past, from my home-town. We had a healthy debate about which teams we liked and why. Our conversation covered several great team that came out of our area high school over the years. However, there was one high school football team that we both agreed on that was truly the best high school football team EVER from my home-town. It was the 1965 Ridgeview Panthers out of Hickory, North Carolina.

The Panthers stood out from every other high school team in the state of North Carolina. The reason they were such standouts was because they not only went undefeated during the entire '64-'65 season (16-0), but they were also UN-SCORED on. So now, we have a team who was perfect in two major ways. That's crazy…right!! It's true. They would later go down in history to be known as "The Untouchables".

As we continued to discuss this team and their unique and rare accomplishments, I asked the gentleman how he thought they were able to pull off such an incredible feat. He proceeded to tell me his thoughts and views as to how it all came about and from this discussion, I took away four major steps that can be used in leadership today. These steps will make leaders even better and more effective and possibly even more likeable!

Chad D. Bumgarner

CONTENTS

PHOTO CREDITS:

Vision

Before we dive into my 4-step methodology for becoming a better leader, we need to discuss an important prerequisite in leadership. This is something that needs to be at the top of every leader's list when trying to lead a group or an organization. Without this very thing, you will have no direction, much like a ship tossed around and lost at sea. A vision, by definition is an aspirational description to what you want the organization to achieve. It's a leader's roadmap for an organization broadcasting what the company wants to become and accomplish. It guides all of the company's initiatives by putting together a solid plan for the employees and leader to adhere to.

In the late 70's there was a young man who had a huge vision of getting a computer into the hands of everyday people. This of course was during a time when computers in the average household was not the norm as it is today. Steve Job's vision was bold and big and he could see it very clearly. However, making it a reality was quite the struggle. Most say that along the way his vision became clouded due to his ego. Did he really hinder the progress or growth of Apple? Probably, but when he was later removed by the board from the company he helped to create, the company itself was much like the ship in the last paragraph that I spoke about, tossed around and lost at sea.

Many years pass and eventually Jobs ended up right back with Apple and helps to make them the comeback kid of this century. Steve had a vision that couldn't be denied and everyone that worked at Apple knew that. No one could stand to work with him or be around him but they all bought into the vision and believed that what he was selling, everyone wanted. Nonetheless, I believe his downfall was in part due to the fact that he made some bad decisions by not constantly going back to his vision and looking at what it would take to make that happen.

There are times when you have to take different routes that you don't too much care for in order to stay true to your vision. That's the point in having one in the first place. Why are you doing what you are doing? Are my decisions aligning with the vision, or are they more self-focused? Am I truly using my vision as a guidepost to all of the tasks that I work on, all of the decisions that I make, and all of the meetings and conference calls that I am apart of?

Let's go one step further, what if your vision was to have a healthy body and mind this year. Well, in order to do that your decisions about what you eat have to line up with having a healthy body right? In addition to this, what you read, think, process and see will aid you in creating a healthy mind as well, right? Anytime, we choose a path that doesn't coincide to the vision, we start to drift away from the prize. Without vision, confusion starts to become more commonplace and not using the guidance that was originally put in place to keep you on track is no longer.

This is one of the most important lessons I had to learn when I decided to focus on leadership and help others enhance their leadership skills so that they can become the leader that people WANT to follow instead of HAVE to follow. In my fifteen plus years in leadership I've learned quite a bit but the lesson on vision is by far one of my most important lessons. In fact, it's so important that it was discussed in the Bible. Proverbs 2:18 says that His people will perish due to lack of vision.

Vision means growth and if you don't have a vision you are basically just getting things done. Management is overseeing daily tasks ensuring that they get completed but vision is evolving and growing an organization or team from what they were, to what the vision states they will become or achieve. A vision usually entails a transformation which is often times a long-term event. If you don't know why you are doing what you are doing, why are you doing it? When I realized this my leadership ability matured tremendously.

I learned about vision as a follower of a leader that left a lot to be desired. He and I started out as engineers on a project and he was exceptionally good at his trade. Eventually he got the nod to become the engineering manager. Now, being a manager and a leader are two different things but one person can effectively wear both hats if done correctly. How many of you know that just because someone is good at what they do, doesn't mean they are qualified to be a good leader? This is when I learned that lesson…...and it was painful for me and everyone else on the team!

Again, he was great at being an engineer but lacked severely in the leadership category. He didn't understand how to lead, impact, influence and empower people. He was very cold to everyone and avoided dialogue as much as possible. However, he enjoyed telling us what we needed to do and how to do it but other ideas and thoughts outside of his own were immediately shot down. He was more of a task manager and just wanted to get things done.

I had no issue with getting things done but the fact was, he wasn't a "task manager", he was the "engineering manager"! He never wanted to discuss training or any kind of self-improvement. We just had to figure it out on our own and it was not to be done during work hours. A lot of us wanted to talk about growth in and outside of the engineering department but he dismissed those talks expeditiously. This was a crucible time in my life and I had to make some tough choices about what was next for me and my career.

Fortunately, I had a friend who was a director in another organization that I spoke to candidly about my situation and he mentioned to me about my manager's vision. I told him that he never spoke about his vision for the team as a whole or individually. He went on to explain the importance of vision and how it helps to keep you on track to reaching your desired results while at the same time giving you the time and ability to grow and evolve. It was then that I learned the importance of having a vision and how it helps to maintain progress and provide constant guidance to everyone.

My good friend continued to show me his vision for his team and the steps that they agreed to take in order to fulfill that vision. I noticed that his team was always vibrant and worked together so well. Everyone was on the same page and my director friend was so awesome at helping his team develop and become the best that they could be. It didn't matter if they needed training or if they needed assistance with creating a career plan, he was there to serve and provide whatever was needed in order to achieve the vision.

This lesson and my good friend are both invaluable to me because when I was finally become a leader, I had success early on because I knew and understood the importance of having a vision and making sure that my team knew it too. One of the things that make a great, high-performing team is synergy. Synergy comes from understanding what your part in the whole is, as well as knowing what the ultimate goal or vision is. When you learn the magnitude of having a vision, over half the battle in leadership is already won!

Now that you see and understand the value of a vision, we can move on to the 4-step methodology that will help catapult your leadership skills to higher heights!

Chad D. Bumgarner

Step One: SET THE STANDARD

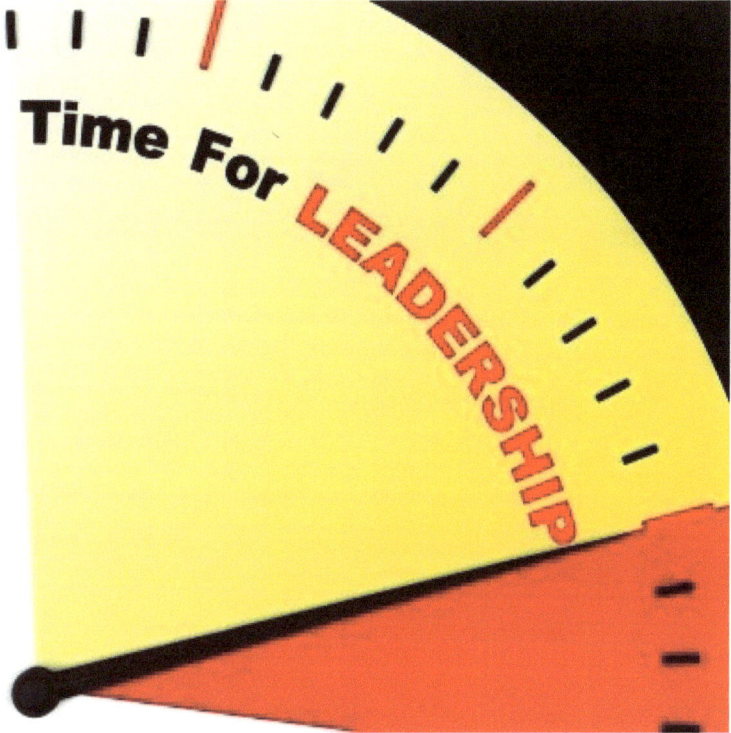

IMAGE COURTESY OF STUART MILES \ FREEDIGITALPHOTOS.NET
"TIME FOR LEADERSHIP MESSAGE REPRESENTING MANAGEMENT AND
ACHIEVEMENT"

Chad D. Bumgarner

SET THE STANDARD

"You have competition every day because you set such high standards for yourself that you have to go out every day and live up to that."

\- Michael Jordan

Chad D. Bumgarner

SETTING THE STANDARD

This is the first step that I took away from the conversation.

The older gentleman explained to me that, over the summer, just before the start of the school year, the head coach called all of the players in for a team meeting. He then went on to say that the coach asked the team if they wanted to win a championship that year. Of course, all of the guys in the meeting were in agreement and wanted to accomplish that goal.

The next question the coach asked was if they were willing to do what it would take to win. Again, the players looked around at each other and agreed that they would do whatever they needed to do to win a championship. The coach and his staff immediately started explaining their vision and goals for the team.

They continued to run down the things in which they would and would not tolerate. They let the players know what would and would not be acceptable. They broke down how practices would be conducted and what was expected of each and every one of them.

What happened here? The coaches **set the standard**. They set the tone for what would eventually be a championship season. They created an atmosphere of change and a championship attitude in the players. This is what leaders should do when coming into a new or existing situation after monitoring the environment for a while.

Leaders need to set the standards for their team or staff so that everyone is on the same page and understands what the vision and goals are for the team.

So many teams are in disarray and productivity is at a minimum mainly because they simply don't know or understand what the vision and the goals are for the team, much less, the company as a whole.

I urge leaders to sit down with their teams and go over these things, making sure that everyone in their group is on the same page. Everybody on the team should be working towards the same goal. Doing this creates unity and eliminates for the most part, confusion and frustration.

When explaining the goals and the vision to the team, please be as clear and concise as possible. It is important that you do this because at the end of the day, you are trying to influence the team or company to "buy in" to the goal/mission and vision. Everyone wants to belong and contribute, but they need to know the how, why, when, and where, etc.

You're probably wondering, "Why should I set the standard?" Well........why not you? You are the leader, the top spot! Everything rises and falls on you so you have to set the standard and the tone.

People will be looking to you for guidance, leadership and understanding. Setting the standard for your team demonstrates your confidence – that you know the direction in which everyone needs to go to obtain the goal. It show that you are clear (and in control) about the plan and the goal. You have to remember that you are creating an environment, a culture and a way of doing things that will result in achieving excellence towards your goals. Setting the standard on a daily basis makes everyone on the team aware of what it is going to take to get things done in the new environment.

It's really not any different than a band's drum major position; knowing exactly where to go and how to direct the band members. All of the band members watch the drum major for directions and instructions. You are the drum major. The leader should set the standard to eliminate chaos and unruly behavior. Setting standards should be a requirement in the beginning to ensure that work and various tasks not contributing to the goal can be eliminated.

REFLECTION TIME

Section One: SETTING THE STANDARD
Questions to answer and reflect on.

Question 1: In this chapter, you read the author's views on
what setting the standard is and what it means. How do
YOU see setting the standard?

_____

_____

_____

_____

_____

_____

_____

_____

_____

_____

_____

_____

_____

_____

Question 2: How do you plan to set the standard where you are?

_____

_____

_____

_____

_____

_____

_____

_____

_____

_____

_____

_____

Question 3: Do you see this step positively or negatively effecting your environment? How?

_____

_____

_____

_____

_____

_____

_____

_____

_____

_____

_____

_____

_____

Question 4: What makes you capable or able to set the standard for your environment?

_____

_____

_____

_____

_____

_____

_____

_____

_____

_____

_____

_____

Question 5: How would you address and resolve any negative feedback or response once you set the standard?

_____

_____

_____

_____

_____

_____

_____

_____

_____

_____

_____

_____

Chad D. Bumgarner

Step Two: TEAMWORK

IMAGE COURTESY OF STUART MILES \ FREEDIGITALPHOTOS.NET
"WORKING TOGETHER ON BLACKBOARD MEANS TEAMWORK AND UNITY
STOCK IMAGE"

Chad D. Bumgarner

Teamwork

"Individual commitment to a group effort – that is what makes a team work, a company work, a society work, a civilization work."

Vince Lombardi

Chad D. Bumgarner

TEAMWORK

In my conversation with the gentleman, he expressed the importance of teamwork and how it was instilled into the players day in and day out. He spoke about how practically everything that the players did reflected teamwork.

The coaching staff insisted on having tutorial sessions after school where the whole team would come in with the tutors They also had the players paired up to study their play books together. Ultimately, they were responsible for each other because, as a team, success and failure was shared. The championship mind frame was enforced on and off the field accordingly. The coaches enforced working together constantly so that the respect for each other's skills, personality and abilities could be earned and trusted.

What am I saying? I'm simply stating that when you work with someone for a period of time, you become more acquainted with them than just on the surface. You understand what they can and can't do. You learn what makes them "tick". More importantly, you learn how to work with them so that their skills, along with yours, can complement each other.

To the team's advantage, the coaches explained the importance of learning their teammate's strengths and weaknesses, so that the players could assist one another in their weaknesses and use their strengths collectively.

Now, in order to create a high-performing, championship team, the coaches knew that the players would go through some changes as a unit before they ended up becoming the team they all wanted to be. These changes that the team would go through would become known as **forming, storming, norming and performing**. A psychologist by the name of Bruce Tuckman came up with this phrase back in 1965 in an article he wrote called, *"Developmental sequence in small groups"*.

Forming is when a specific group of individuals are brought together for the first time and are excited about the goal and eager to get started. Everything is vague temporarily but enthusiasm is still high.

Storming is when conflict arises due to the job duties and responsibilities being vague. Personalities and working styles aren't fully understood by the team yet. The team is trying to get things done but people are overlapping with their roles and it causes a bit of friction. Individual cliques start to form and take shape.

Norming happens when guidance and responsibilities are clear, communicated and understood by everyone on the team. Every individual knows what the boundaries are and behavior is at an acceptable level. Team members are now comfortable with their duties and one another.

Performing is when the team has finally worked out all of the kinks. The team is now executing at a high-performance capacity and everyone is confident in what they're doing as well as their team mate. At this stage in the game, everyone knows their assignment and requires minimum supervision from leadership.

I strongly suggest the teamwork approach and philosophy in the workplace. When leaders either create a team or inherit an existing team, not only should they understand Bruce Tuckman's process I just explained, they should also be thinking about the following steps as well:

> ➤ Give the team the vision and the goals that you want them to have (get them to buy in to your direction)

> ➤ How can I establish trust with this team?

> ➤ Implement the S.W.O.T analysis (Strengths, Weaknesses, Opportunities, Threats)

> ➤ Incorporate trust, transparency and empowerment within the team

Leaders should first and foremost, explain to their team what the vision and the goals are. I can't emphasize this enough.

For the head coach of the Panthers, the vision was to create an atmosphere of championship caliber. His vision for his team was to create a mindset where everything they did and said, contributed to their work towards being champions. Their goal was to win the championship. I don't think you can get much clearer than that! Your vision and goal will probably be a bit different, but the method/approach should still be the same. You need to be clear and keep it as simple as possible so that everyone understands.

As a leader, it's imperative that you work with your team to know and understand everyone's strengths and weaknesses, opportunities and threats.

Image courtesy of 89studio \ FreeDigitalPhotos.net "Businessman With Idea Concept"

- **Strengths** = what is everyone's expertise
- **Weaknesses =** what is it that everyone may need more training on?
- **Opportunities** = what are some avenues in which everyone can grow and achieve?
- **Threats** = what are some things in everyone that could potentially harm the team?

This is popularly known as the *S.W.O.T* analysis. This is knowledge that is crucial to you as a leader because you will need to know how to use your team members wisely and effectively. Understanding how to use the S.W.O.T analysis and incorporate it into your team and teamwork will drastically increase camaraderie, trust and productivity.

Teamwork also fosters a bond between team members and the leader which can prove to be very beneficial to the corporation as well. Teams that are cohesive and can collaborate very well together are more productive than teams that are the opposite.

Why is that? Teams of this magnitude have created a level of trust and transparency with one another. Each member understands their purpose and what they bring to the table. Teams like these have learned how to effectively communicate with one another. They understand accountability for themselves and for each other. Teams that understand teamwork know how to break down a big project and delegate assignments based upon their expertise.

For example, let's say you have John, whose strength is technical writing and Rich, whose strength is net computer networking. There's a project that requires someone to investigate and document a network connectivity issue. Well, as a leader, you would know that Rick would be the best candidate to handle the networking issue because of his skills. Rick knows that once he has investigated and resolved the matter, a write up will have to be done about what happened and how it was fixed. He would then need to work with John to document the issue and present the information to the manager.

Chad D. Bumgarner

REFLECTION TIME

Section Two: TEAMWORK

Questions to answer and reflect on.

Question 1: Why is teamwork so vital to the success of a goal?

Question 2: How will you incorporate teamwork so that you and your team are successful in accomplishing your goals?

_____

_____

_____

_____

_____

_____

_____

_____

_____

_____

_____

_____

Question 3: Is synergy a necessity to having a high-performing team? If so, why?

_____

_____

_____

_____

_____

_____

_____

_____

_____

_____

_____

_____

_____

Question 4: As a leader, how do you plan to analyze your team and make it better?

_____

_____

_____

_____

_____

_____

_____

_____

_____

_____

_____

Question 5: As a leader, how would you go about finding the strengths, weaknesses, opportunities and threats that lie within your team in order to make them better?

_____

_____

_____

_____

_____

_____

_____

_____

_____

_____

_____

_____

Chad D. Bumgarner

Step Three: ADAPT

Image courtesy of Grant Cochrane / FreeDigitalPhotos.net "Plan A Plan B A Chalkboard"

Chad D. Bumgarner

ADAPT

'Adapt and overcome' is my new motto.

\- Jack Osbourne

Chad D. Bumgarner

ADAPT

Every team or company comes to a fork in the road where they much decide to either adapt to change or remain the same, which could be detrimental to their existence.

As leaders, when necessary, we must all learn when and how to adapt and change for the best. Remaining the same or "standing still" could potentially cause you to become ancient history and lose strong footing in the ever changing global market place.

The coach for the Panthers understood very well about adapting. He understood that being the best meant learning how to prepare for all types of situations to ensure that all, or at least most of his bases were covered. For example, the Panthers were about to play a team that focused mainly on running the football. The Panther's head coach taught and prepared his team to defend the opponents running scheme.

On game day, the Panthers were ready to play this team who took pride in their running game. There was one problem though. The team that loved to run came out passing the ball! The Panthers were initially stunned and caught off guard. Remember what I said earlier about the Panther's head coach. He understood how to adapt and prepare for various situations to ensure that most of his bases were covered. After about the third straight completion, the Panthers called a timeout to regroup. The coach quickly made the proper adjustments that would remedy the problem they had encountered. In order for the coach to know what to do and what adjustments to make, he had to know his player's strengths and weaknesses. He knew which players had the ability to play effectively against the passing scheme of the opponents. The adjustments that were made helped the Panthers and they eventually continued on to win the game. This skill is important for leaders to learn –

understand that when situations require change, adapt with transparency, and convey clear, definitive decisions to the team about the changes and why.

Leaders have to step back sometimes and look ahead for vision and preparation. Sometimes we can see change coming and sometimes it will hit us out of the blue. Having the knowledge to look at the present and prepare for the future will be crucial to a leader's success. Being able to perfect the art of adapting will separate the good leaders from the great leaders.

In some instances, this part of leadership hurts a lot of leaders because of pride. Some leaders refuse to believe that their way isn't working or that their vision or plan may need to be revised. Catastrophes , in most situations, will more than likely occur and the brunt of the suffering will belong to the team or company.

Understanding this skill and knowing when and how to use it can ultimately make or break you as a leader. A great example of understanding how to adapt would be the Marines. This great military branch of the U.S. Armed Forces pride themselves in knowing what to do even when they don't know what to do! In other words, they learn to think and react quickly on their feet and improvise if the initial plan is not working. This trait is what can keep you alive in business and in life.

ADAPT!!

LEARN IT!!

UNDERSTAND IT!!

PERFECT IT!!

REFLECTION TIME:

Section three: ADAPT

Questions to answer and reflect upon

Question 1: How would you handle having to adapt? (EX: new plan of action, new employee to the team, department consolidation, etc.)

_____

_____

_____

_____

_____

_____

_____

_____

_____

_____

_____

_____

_____

Question 2: Why is adapting so hard for teams and even some leaders to do?

_____

_____

_____

_____

_____

_____

_____

_____

_____

_____

_____

_____

Question 3: Why is knowing how and when to adapt so important?

_____

_____

_____

_____

_____

_____

_____

_____

_____

_____

_____

_____

Question 4: As a leader, if the time came to adapt to a new system, a new employee, a new business plan, etc., how would you respond to the potential negative feedback and responses to the situation?

_____

_____

_____

_____

_____

_____

_____

_____

_____

_____

_____

_____

Question 5: How will you educate your team on how to adapt? Will you be receptive to all feedback or will you go at it your way?

_____

_____

_____

_____

_____

_____

_____

_____

_____

_____

_____

Chad D. Bumgarner

Step Four: RELEVANCE

IMAGE COURTESY OF STUART MILES \ FREEDIGITALPHOTOS.NET
"OBJECTIVES ON CHALKBOARD REPRESENTS AIMS GOALS AND
ACHIEVABLE TA STOCK IMAGE"

Chad D. Bumgarner

RELEVANCE

"Empirical interest will be in the facts so far as they are relevant to the solution of these problems?

- Talcott Parsons

Chad D. Bumgarner

RELEVANCE

This is what it all comes down to. This step helps keep us focused throughout the entire process. This pretty much wraps up all of the other steps with a pretty little bow on top!

Everything you do, all of your planning, meetings, scheduling, hard work, and limitless efforts should all be relevant to the goal.

Let's quickly review what the coach did. First, he set the standard with the players in their first meeting before the new season started. He worked on creating an environment and a mindset of championship caliber. He laid down the foundation for how the team would move forward into the season with how they would do things.

The next thing he did was incorporate the importance of teamwork on and off the field. He emphasized the importance of it and how it can strengthen the team as a whole. Coach understood how crucial it was to know how and when to adapt when times called for it. He educated his staff and players about the changes and why they were needed. He also used the S.W.O.T analysis to understand his players and how best to use them when faced with various situations in any given game. All of these things come down to the last step which is being relevant. Everything that the coach, his staff and his players did was all relevant to the goal which was to win a championship. They changed their way of doing things.

They changed their mindset. They spent the entire season doing things they had never done before in order to achieve the one thing they had never accomplished. This method can work for any leader out there who's willing to go the extra mile and change the "business as usual" mindset. This method can be implemented in either a brand new team that's being put together or even an existing team. The only way that it will ever be successful for you is by believing in the system and then getting your team to buy in to the system as well.

As a leader you constantly have to stop and do an analysis with your team to see how things are going. You need to make sure that everyone is on task and working on their part to fulfill the goal. You should ensure that every task, every plan, every meeting is relevant towards the goal that you are trying to accomplish. In doing this, you cut down on miscellaneous activities that usually happen and can potentially take you off track or derail your project or mission altogether. This method is easy and simple to use so again, let's recap quickly.

S – Standard (set it!)
T – Teamwork (incorporate it!)
A – Adapt (Learn it! Understand it! Perfect it!)
R – Relevant (Everything you do MUST be towards the goal!)

Using this S.T.A.R method will make you a STAR wherever you lead. I really believe that this book can help you become a better, more effective and efficient leader. Take the time to think about each step and visualize how you plan to execute this method wherever you are now.

I wish you all the best in your future endeavors!

Remember....Great leadership = Great results...."How are you leading?"

Chad D. Bumgarner

REFLECTION TIME:

Section Four: RELEVANCE

Questions to answer and reflect on

Question 1: Why is relevance so important to accomplishing a goal?

_____

_____

_____

_____

_____

_____

_____

_____

_____

_____

_____

_____

Question 2: What should be relevant to you as a leader pertaining to your goals and plans?

_____

_____

_____

_____

_____

_____

_____

_____

_____

_____

_____

_____

Question 3: What things can you do to keep everyone's actions on the team relevant to the goal?

_____

_____

_____

_____

_____

_____

_____

_____

_____

_____

_____

_____

Question 4: How would you get your team to understand how important it is that all of their actions should be relevant towards the goal?

_____

_____

_____

_____

_____

_____

_____

_____

_____

_____

_____

_____

Question 5: What steps would you take in order to keep yourself and your action relevant to the goal?

_____

_____

_____

_____

_____

_____

_____

_____

_____

_____

_____

_____

_____

Chad D. Bumgarner

Conclusion

Let's be honest here.......this book is not the "end all be all" for and about leadership. It is a high level attempt at helping leaders become better and more impactful at leading teams and creating better environments so that success is inevitable. The underlining yet subtle stitch that weaves the entire methodology together is communication.

A leader must be able to communicate extremely well with their teams. A huge part of communicating is listening. You cannot lead if you cannot listen. Over the course of implementing these steps I've created, pay close attention to the feedback and response of your team. Body language is just as important as what is verbally being said.

In addition to reading the book, reflect deeply upon your leadership style, traits and characteristics. A lot of times when we evaluate ourselves we are not as honest as we should be. The more honest you are with your self-assessment, the better chance you have at understanding where you are and what you need to change.

The Marines adhere to a phrase that I think is a great motto that all leaders should incorporate into their leadership. The phrase is "Ductos Exemplo," which means lead by example. All leaders should aspire to do such a thing.

Chad D. Bumgarner

Thoughts about the Book from others......

I think that the "Playbook" is an intriguing and imaginative way to get individuals to think about what it means to be a leader and what leader behaviors are important, e.g., setting standards, building teams, creating sustainable change, and being mission driven (relevant). Well done!

Dr. Thomas E. Kail, Professor of Leadership and Applied Studies, Mercer University

I believe that Chad's Playbook To Effective Leadership is the perfect book to use in leadership retreats or for an individual leader looking to enhance their leadership skills. I appreciate how Chad's storyline about the undefeated football team is complimentary to the 4-step S.T.A.R method of leadership. His straightforward approach of leadership development kept me engaged and eager to write down my countless thoughts in the reflections area provided at the end of each section. I gained considerable knowledge and motivation to become a better leader after completing Chad's Playbook To Effective Leadership! This book is a must-have resource for leaders to add to their library.

Rhonda Sherrod, Development Office Administrator, Atlanta Speech School

The S.T.A.R principle, presented in this book, serves as a practical and effective guideline for achieving team success. I recommend this book to all leaders wanting to lead their teams more effectively.

Denard Ash, Project Manager, Ciena

Chad D. Bumgarner

ABOUT THE AUTHOR

Chad D. Bumgarner
www.Chadbumgarner.co

Chad D. Bumgarner

Chad is one of the most upbeat and passionate speakers out today but he's so much more than that. He is also a team - building facilitator and a leadership development coach with the background and experience to provide people with quality information that will get them the results they need.

Chad has spent over twenty years working in team settings and being in leadership positions so he understands fully what it takes to lead and build high performance teams. He enjoys talking to up-and-coming as well as seasoned leaders about what it takes to be an effective, efficient and ethical leader. He believes that leadership is about influence but the key is to use your influence correctly so that you and your team are successful.

Chad is committed to bringing the best out of every crowd he speaks to. He has a fiery desire to educate, stimulate and stretch leaders to think outside of the box and become a better and more engaging leader. He is constantly tweaking and working on new ways, methodologies and strategies in order to provide stellar services that meet or exceed the client's expectations.

If you want Chad to come out and hold a training session, or even to speak to your team or group, please inquire about his availability as well as other specific services you would like for him to provide at *info@chadbumgarner.co*

"If your actions inspire others to dream more, learn more, do more and become more, you are a leader."

- John Quincy Adams

Chad D. Bumgarner

Other Writings by
   Chad D. Bumgarner

CHAD'S PLAYBOOK
FOR
EFFECTIVE
FATHERING

The book gives insight to the importance of balance and a solid foundation in a child's life. It shows the effects of children growing up with an absentee father.

Available now at amazon.com and createspace.com

2015©
ISBN 9-781937-118525

Chad D. Bumgarner

www.ingramcontent.com/pod-product-compliance
Lightning Source LLC
Chambersburg PA
CBHW042025210326
41519CB00051B/142